*10956*

574.5
PRI

Pringle, Laurence P

Estuaries; where
rivers meet the
sea

# ESTUARIES
## WHERE RIVERS MEET THE SEA

# Estuaries
## Where Rivers Meet the Sea

# by Laurence Pringle

MACMILLAN PUBLISHING CO., INC.
New York
COLLIER MACMILLAN PUBLISHERS
London

Macmillan Publishing Co., Inc.,
866 Third Avenue, New York, N.Y. 10022
Collier-Macmillan Canada Ltd.

Library of Congress catalog card number: 72–86506

Printed in the United States of America

10 9 8 7 6 5 4 3 2

---

Library of Congress Cataloging in Publication Data

Pringle, Laurence P
  Estuaries; where rivers meet the sea.

  SUMMARY: Introduces in text and photographs the physical characteristics and plant and animal inhabitants of one of earth's most valuable ecosystems—the estuary.
    1. Estuarine ecology—Juvenile literature.
[1. Estuarine ecology. 2. Ecology] I. Title.
QH541.5.E8P75      574.5′2636      72–86506
ISBN 0–02–775300–X

---

For Diane Amussen

## ABOUT THIS BOOK

An estuary is a kind of ecosystem—a place in nature with all of its living and nonliving parts. Ecosystems are all around us. Some are big, some are little. The planet earth is one ecosystem, a rotting log is another. Forests, ponds, and back yards are also ecosystems.

This book introduces estuary ecosystems. Estuaries are found wherever there is a mixing of fresh river water and salty sea water. There are about nine hundred estuaries along the coasts of the United States. They are homes for many kinds of animals, including shore birds, fiddler crabs, oysters, and young ocean fish. Estuaries are among the most valuable ecosystems on earth.

Estuaries are places of shifting tides and deep mud. Some parts are hard to explore without a boat. But you can see estuary life near beaches and along the edges of salt marshes. Through your own observations and through the pages of this book, you can get to know the fascinating ecosystems where rivers meet the sea.

**A**S RIVERS FLOW to the sea, their fresh water mixes with the salty sea water. Sometimes fresh water also seeps from underground all along a seashore. The places where fresh water and sea water mix are called estuaries.

Estuaries are homes for many kinds of animals. Long-legged herons and egrets wade in the water. Gulls and terns swoop overhead. Scallops, oysters, crabs, and fish live underwater. Many kinds of ocean fish spend part of their lives in estuaries. Without estuaries, these fish could not survive. Estuaries are among the liveliest and most valuable ecosystems on earth.

When the tide goes out, birds hunt for food on the beaches and mud flats of estuaries.

Usually an estuary is called a bay, sound, harbor, or lagoon. Along the coasts of Norway and Alaska, the deep, narrow estuaries are called fjords. An estuary can be small or it can be a huge body of water. One of the biggest is Chesapeake Bay, on the east coast of the United States. It is 195 miles long and covers almost three million acres. About 150 rivers and smaller streams carry fresh water into Chesapeake Bay.

The bay was once a wide river valley. Then, about ten thousand years ago, the sea level rose. Salt water filled part of the valley. Scientists call Chesapeake Bay a "drowned" river valley. Many other estuaries, including fjords, are also drowned valleys.

Chesapeake Bay is a huge estuary on the eastern coast of the United States. In it, fresh water from a hundred and fifty rivers and other streams mixes with salt water from the Atlantic Ocean. The bay was once a big valley. It filled with water when the sea level rose about ten thousand years ago.

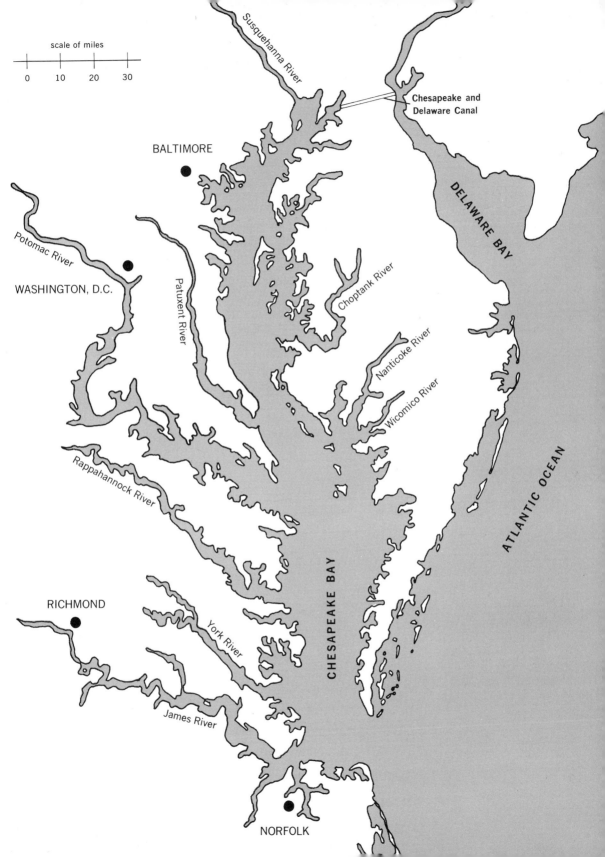

scale of miles

0    10    20    30

Susquehanna River

Chesapeake and
Delaware Canal

BALTIMORE

DELAWARE BAY

Potomac River

WASHINGTON, D.C.

Patuxent River

Choptank River

Nanticoke River

Wicomico River

ATLANTIC OCEAN

Rappahannock River

CHESAPEAKE BAY

RICHMOND

York River

James River

NORFOLK

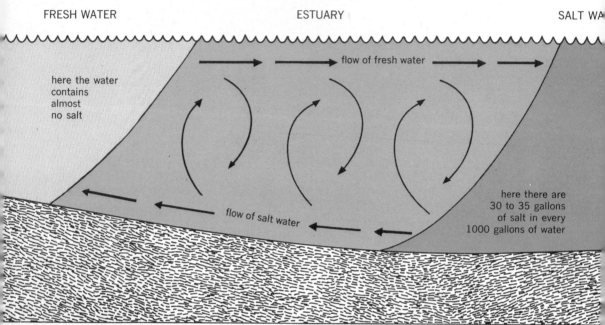

FRESH WATER ESTUARY SALT WA

here the water
contains
almost
no salt

flow of fresh water

flow of salt water

here there are
30 to 35 gallons
of salt in every
1000 gallons of water

River and tidal currents mix in an estuary.
But salt water is heavier than fresh water, so
water near the bottom is saltier than on top.

An estuary provides many different living places for plants and animals. In some parts of an estuary the water may be two hundred feet deep. In others it is shallow. Grasses and other marsh plants grow in shallow water at the edge of estuaries.

The amount of salt in the water also varies. Where the estuary empties into the ocean, there are 30 to 35 gallons of salt in every 1,000 gallons of water. Up the river, at the other end of the estuary, the water contains almost no salt. In between the water gets saltier as it gets closer to the open sea.

Animal life in the estuary is affected by the amount of salt in the water. Starfish need the saltiness of the sea. They live only in the ocean or in the saltiest part of the estuary. Other kinds of animals need less salt. Some sea worms, crabs, and oysters can live where there are only five gallons of salt in a thousand gallons of water. They are found where the water is almost fresh, far from the sea.

Salt water is heavier than fresh water. It sinks in the estuary, so the water near the bottom is saltier than on top. This affects living things too. Some sea animals live far up the estuary. They dwell on the bottom where the water is salty, but could not survive in the fresh water near the surface.

In the springtime, rivers are full of rainwater and melted snow. Great amounts of fresh water flow into the estuary. It becomes less salty. During these times, some of the fish, crabs, and other animals may move closer to the sea. Clams and other animals that move very little close their shells. They live off stored food. They may die if a flood of fresh water lasts a long time and all of their stored food is used up.

Rivers carry less water in the summer. The entire estuary becomes more salty and salt water reaches farther up the river. Sea animals also swim, crawl, or drift farther up the river.

All year round, rivers and smaller streams carry mud, silt, and other sediments into the estuary. Some of these sediments go out into the sea. Others settle to the bottom and gradually make the estuary more shallow. The sediments may be a hundred feet deep in the deepest channels. Sediments also build up in shallow areas. Sand and silt are trapped among plant stems in the salt marshes and slowly raise the level of the marshes.

Rivers also carry food—bits of leaves and other plant parts—into the estuary. More food is provided by tiny plants called algae that drift in the water. Other kinds of algae grow in the mud and on the stalks of salt marsh grasses.

Horseshoe crabs feed on detritus and other food they find on the estuary bottom. These animals are not really crabs; they are more closely related to spiders. During the spring and summer they crawl to shallow water, with the smaller males clinging to the females. After the crabs mate they return to the sea for another year.

When the tide goes out, bits of detritus are carried out of the salt marshes and into the rest of the estuary. Fish retreat with the tides.

The greatest source of food for all estuary animals is the grasses themselves. Some are eaten by grasshoppers, other insects, and mud crabs. But most of the grass is eaten after it dies. Tiny plants called bacteria and fungi feed on dead grasses and break them down into smaller pieces. The bits of dead grass are called detritus.

When the tide comes in, water fills the creeks and spreads across low parts of the marshes. Fish feed along the creek edges and in the marshes.

Twice a day the tides wash into the marshes and out again. Bits of detritus are carried off by the tidal currents. Detritus spreads all over the estuary with the mixing of the tides and the river currents. Together with algae, detritus is the most abundant and most important food in the estuary.

The water of an estuary is like vegetable soup. Many estuary animals eat this soup. Oysters, clams, and mussels strain food from the water. They are called filter feeders. An oyster pumps eight gallons of water through its gills in an hour. Detritus, algae, and tiny animals are caught in the oyster's gills, then pushed into its mouth.

Other animals eat dead bits of grass they find in the mud. Snails scrape detritus and algae from the bottom and from grass stalks. Mullet also eat detritus. These silvery fish filter it out of the water and also from mouthfuls of bottom mud. One way or another, plant-eating animals get energy from the plants they eat. They also get nutrients such as nitrogen from plants.

Then the plant-eating animals become food themselves. Mussels, clams, and crabs are eaten by raccoons and mink along the edge of the estuary. Snails, crabs, shrimp, and fish are snatched from the water by birds. Plant-eating animals are also eaten by many kinds of large fish. The nutrients and some of the energy from the bodies of plant-eating animals become part of other living things.

Snails called periwinkles (above) scrape bits of food from plant stalks. Mussels (right) are filter feeders, sifting detritus from the water around them. They close their shells when the tide goes out.

When a fish, bird, or crab dies, its energy and nutrients are not lost. Some of its body may be eaten by another animal. Or it may decay, and some of its energy is then taken up by bacteria. Some of a dead animal's nutrients are let go in the water or mud. The ever-mixing estuary waters help keep nutrients from being carried out to sea. These valuable materials may be taken into the roots of a plant and later become part of a leaf. Then they are available as food for an animal once more. The estuary plants and shifting tides add to the vegetable soup every day.

Estuaries are not easy places to explore. One minute you may be fighting your way through tall, sharp-edged grasses, the next you may be up to your waist in gooey mud. Even so, from the edge of a salt marsh or from a boat, there are many fascinating things to see.

Here the tide has gone out and exposed the muddy banks of a creek. Fiddler crabs hunt for bits of food in the mud. They get energy and nutrients from the food. An estuary is a "nutrient trap," where minerals and other nutrients are used again and again by plants and animals.

Look at the salt marsh grasses. They are called cordgrasses because people once twisted similar tough-leaved grasses into thin ropes or cords. The scientific name for cordgrasses is *Spartina,* from the Greek word for cord. The *Spartinas* are among the most valuable plants on earth. Most rooted plants cannot survive in salt water. *Spartinas* thrive in it. They provide shelter and food for many estuary animals in areas washed by tides, whipped by sea winds, and burned by the sun.

One kind of *Spartina* grows only two feet high. Layers of dead leaves cover the ground beneath the living green ones because only the highest tides reach this high marsh. Taller cordgrass grows near the water on creek banks. It may reach a height of ten feet. Snails called periwinkles scrape algae from the ground and from the *Spartina* stalks. The tides flood this low area twice a day. Dead leaves are carried off, so there is only bare mud beneath the living plants.

The black-necked stilt hunts for insects and snails in shallow water and among the short cordgrasses of salt marshes.

The tallest Spartinas, or
cordgrasses, grow along
creek banks. Great blue
herons prowl along the
edges of these creeks,
hunting fish and crabs.

Fiddler crabs scuttle about on the mud. Each male fiddler has one front claw that is much bigger than the others. It is easy to understand how fiddler crabs were named when you see a male waving its big claw back and forth, back and forth, like someone playing a violin. Males battle with their big claws. They tug and yank at one another, and sometimes the loser is thrown through the air. At mating time, the males wave their brightly colored "fiddle bows" at females.

Fiddler crabs dig deep burrows in the mud beneath the tall cordgrasses. As the tide rises, they crawl into their burrows and make a door of mud pellets. When the tide falls, the fiddlers come out and roam through the marsh, looking for morsels of food uncovered or left by the tidal currents.

Here two male fiddler crabs are battling with their big claws. At mating time the big claws are brightly colored, and the males wave them at female fiddlers.

Each fiddler crab scoops up bits of food in its claws and puts them in its mouth. A male uses its one small front claw; the female eats with two. Bristles in the crab's mouth sort out food of the size and kind it likes. Then the crab spits the rest into a claw and puts it back in the mud.

Millions of fiddlers may live on an acre of salt marsh. As they move they cause the grass to rustle as though a breeze were blowing. Curlews, clapper rails, and other birds catch and eat fiddlers. So do purple marsh crabs. These large crabs lurk just inside their burrows. They wait for a fiddler to pass by, then drag it underground. Purple marsh crabs also eat pieces of *Spartina*, clipping them off with their claws and grinding them into bits with their mouthparts.

Female fiddler crabs eat with both of their front claws. The male fiddler crab (left) picks up food with the small claw opposite its "fiddle bow."

When tides flood the marshes, animals from other parts of the estuary swim or crawl among the grass stems. Striped bass, flounders, squid, and blue crabs hunt for mud crabs and fiddler crabs, worms, and other plant-eating animals.

Pools of water remain in low spots when the tide goes out. In them and in tidal creeks you may see some of the small fishes of the estuary. They have fascinating names: killifish, silversides, sheepshead minnow, mummichog, anchovy, top minnow, stickleback. Mummichogs are a kind of killifish. They and top minnows eat many of the young mosquitoes that wriggle about in the tide pools.

The names of estuary fish vary from place to place. A fish has one name in one estuary and another farther along the coast. Fishermen call the same fish menhaden, pogies, mossbunkers, and fatbacks. Striped bass are also known as rockfish, linesiders, greenheads, and squidhounds.

Sticklebacks (top) are small fish that feed on tiny crustaceans, young fish, and fish eggs. They live in tidal creeks and pools along with mummichogs (bottom), a kind of killifish.

Beyond the edge of the marsh at low tide, you may see eelgrass waving in the currents beneath the surface. It is related to pondweeds but is called a grass because of its long, narrow leaves. Unlike the cordgrasses, eelgrass must always be covered by salt water in order to stay alive. On and near the eelgrass live plants and animals that have the same need. Algae grow on eelgrass stems. Detritus particles cling to them. Worms, mollusks (shelled animals), and crustaceans (crablike animals) feed on this plant food.

Eelgrass is a favorite food of small dark sea geese

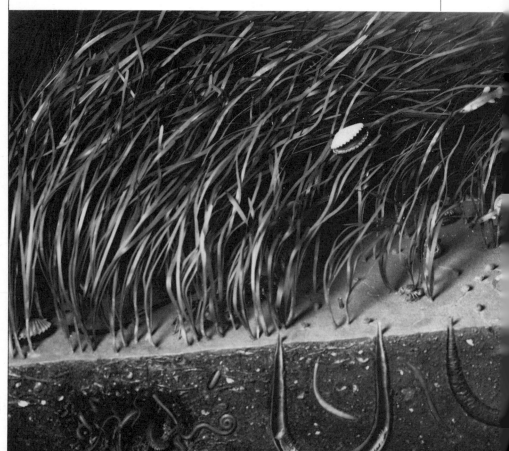

called brant. Together with millions of other geese and ducks, brant spend their winters in northern estuaries along the Atlantic and Pacific coasts. They feed at low tide, dipping their heads underwater and eating eelgrass roots.

Eelgrass thrives in the shallow waters of many estuaries. This exhibit at The American Museum of Natural History shows some of the life in an eelgrass meadow—worms burrowing in the mud, snails and several kind of crabs crawling on the bottom, killifish swimming near a scallop. (Courtesy of The American Museum of Natural History)

25

Many animals live in underwater eelgrass meadows. Hermit crabs crawl about, dragging the snail shells which they take over and carry with them for protection. Eels, flounders, and other fish come in from deeper water to hunt. The flounders lie on the bottom. Their flat bodies squirm into the mud and sand until they are almost completely hidden. There they wait for the shrimps and crabs they like to eat.

Scallops also live in the eelgrass meadows. Rows of bright blue eyes peer out from between their open shells. When a scallop senses danger, it rapidly flaps the two halves of its shell open and shut. Jets of water squirt out and the scallop takes off on a wild dash to safety.

Two rows of bright round eyes peer out of a scallop's open shell. When the shell is open, dozens of tiny tentacles detect chemicals in the water, and alert the scallop to enemies. Unlike oysters, scallops can move about on the bottom, and can even jet through the water to escape danger.

Oysters are the most common mollusks in many estuaries. Unlike scallops and mussels, oysters cannot move about. Only the tiny young oysters, called larvae, are free in the water. Millions of them swim and drift with the tides for about two weeks after they are let go in the water by female oysters. They spread all over the estuary. Many are eaten.

When the larvae settle to the bottom they attach themselves to a solid object, if they are lucky. Many settle down in the mud and die. Great numbers of young oysters glue themselves to the shells of live or dead oysters. There they begin to develop into adults. They never travel again.

Oyster beds are spread all over the estuary bottom, and are homes for fish, crabs, worms, and many other animals.

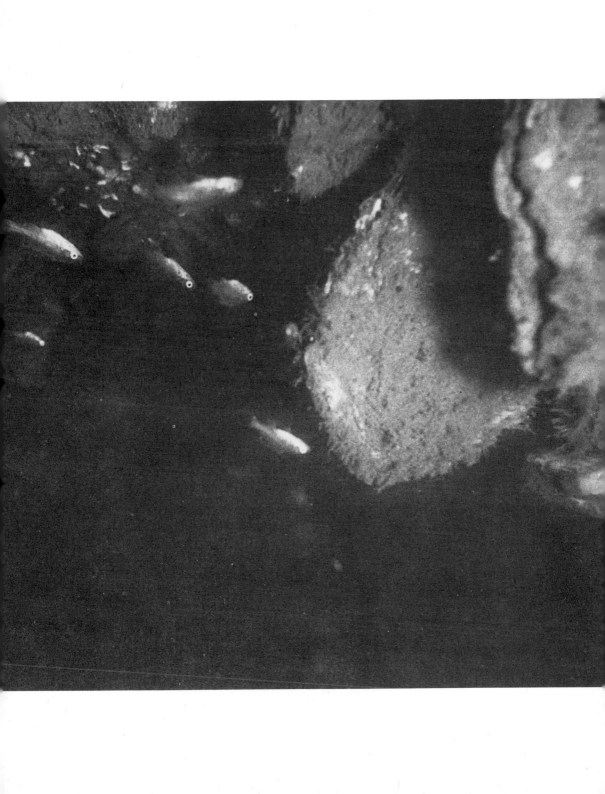

Many animals eat oysters. Starfish pull them apart with powerful sucking disks on their arms. Oysters are safe from starfish in the parts of the estuary where the water is not very salty. Another oyster enemy is a small yellow snail called the oyster drill. With its filelike tongue, the snail begins to cut a hole in an oyster's shell. The oyster drill also produces a chemical that eats away the shell and makes the hole deeper. Eventually the snail bores all the way through the oyster shell and eats the defenseless animal inside.

Oyster drills need at least nine gallons of salt in every thousand gallons of water in order to survive. Oysters can live in less salty water. So the oysters that live near the upstream end of an estuary are free from attacks by oyster drills.

The snails called oyster drills settle upon oyster shells (top left) and file holes through them with their tongue. The picture at the bottom left shows several adult starfish invading a bed of two-year-old oysters. The five oysters at the right are growing on a scallop shell.

Another enemy of oysters is a fish called the black drum. It grabs oysters whole and crushes their shells with powerful teeth. Then the drum swallows the oysters and spits out the shell fragments.

Although many animals eat oysters, these mollusks survive because each female produces millions of young each year. Oysters grow in clusters called beds all over the estuary bottom, except where the sediments are deep. Wherever they live, oysters provide homes for other animals. Worms, snails, crabs, sea anemones, and jellyfish live in oyster beds. Some animals attach themselves to oyster shells. Others hide in between. Some creatures, including a worm and a tiny crab, even live inside oysters. Scientists have found more than three hundred kinds of animals living in or near oyster beds.

Sea anemones sometimes attach themselves to oyster shells. Their waving tentacles sting and catch small animals that swim nearby.

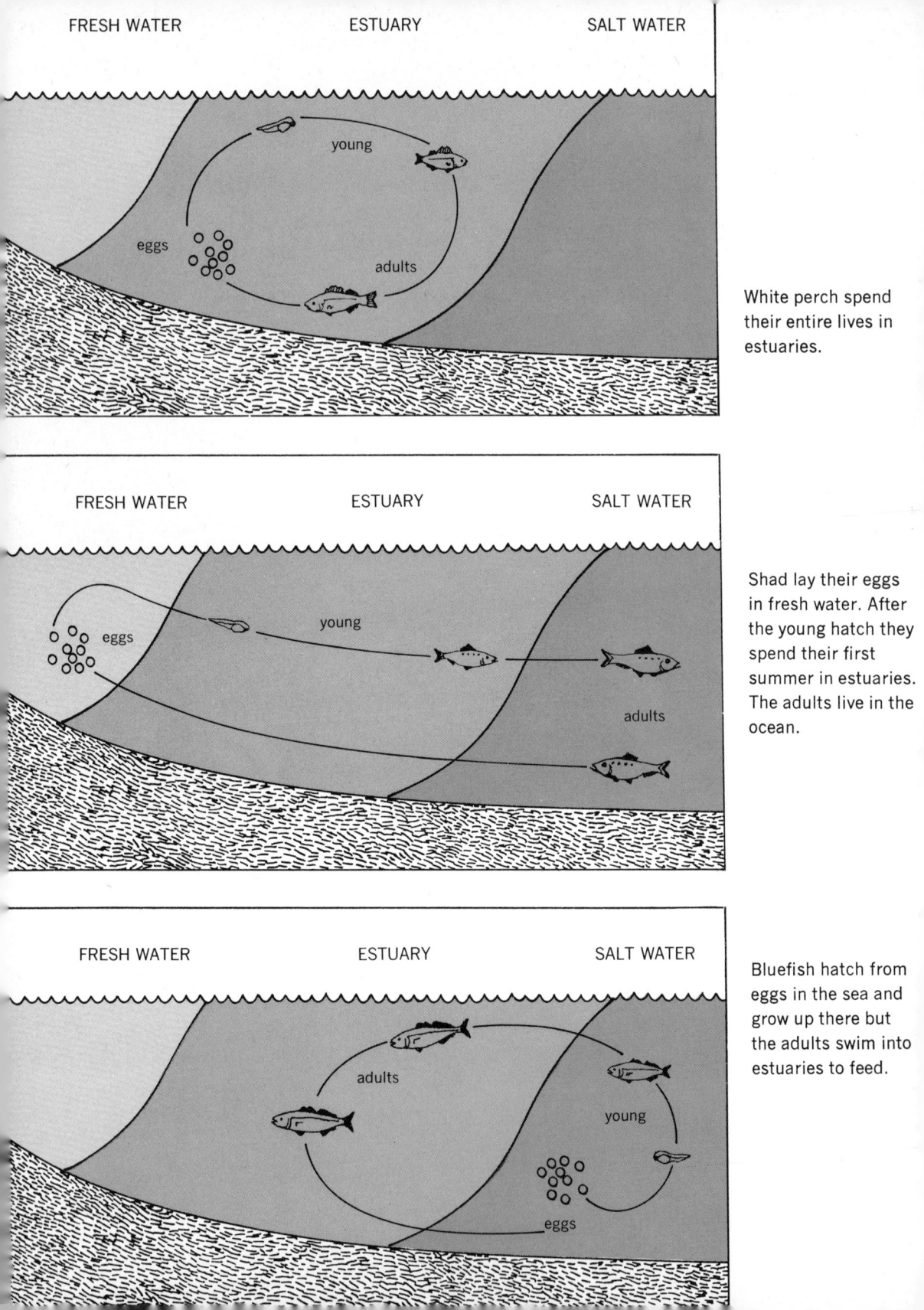

FRESH WATER    ESTUARY    SALT WATER

young

eggs

adults

White perch spend their entire lives in estuaries.

FRESH WATER    ESTUARY    SALT WATER

eggs

young

adults

Shad lay their eggs in fresh water. After the young hatch they spend their first summer in estuaries. The adults live in the ocean.

FRESH WATER    ESTUARY    SALT WATER

adults

young

eggs

Bluefish hatch from eggs in the sea and grow up there but the adults swim into estuaries to feed.

Above the oyster beds swim fish by the millions. They use estuary waters in several different ways. White perch spend their entire lives in estuaries. Young bluefish and menhaden hatch from eggs in the sea. After they grow to be adults, they swim to estuaries to feed. Young croakers also hatch from eggs in the sea, but they are swept into estuaries by the tides and grow up there.

Salmon swim upstream through estuaries and on to fresh water where they spawn (reproduce). Shad also swim upstream to fresh water and spawn, but their young soon swim downstream to the estuary. They spend their first summer there.

Estuaries are nurseries for many other kinds of young ocean fish. The fish are safe from some of their ocean enemies and food is plentiful. Little menhaden, croakers, and mullet eat detritus, algae, and tiny animals. Small crustaceans, oyster larvae, and worms are eaten by young flounders, herrings, striped bass, and tarpon. Estuaries are also nurseries for young shrimp and blue crabs.

Fish depend on estuaries in many different ways. The drawings on the opposite page show how estuaries are important to three different kinds of fish.

After a time, many of the young ocean animals leave the estuaries. They go to sea and spread out along the coast. Half of all the striped bass caught along the Atlantic Coast hatched from eggs in Chesapeake Bay. In fact, two out of every three kinds of valuable food fish netted along the Atlantic Coast spend part of their lives in estuaries. Half of the seafood harvested along the Pacific Coast also depends on estuaries.

Whether you live close to an estuary or far away, your life is tied to salt marshes and eelgrass meadows. Whenever you eat scallops, oysters, clams, sole, or many other kinds of seafood, your body receives energy and nutrients from estuaries. Even tuna, which are caught far out in the ocean, contain energy and nutrients from estuaries. They eat menhaden, herrings, and other fish that spend part of their lives in estuaries.

Fish that are caught all along the coast usually spend part of their lives in estuaries.

Everyone is tied to estuaries, whether they eat seafood or not. For example, menhaden are seldom eaten by people. But they are used in pet and livestock food, and in fertilizers. Oil from menhaden is used in making paint, varnish, ink, lipstick, soap, insect spray, and in tanning leather. Whoever uses these products is also making use of estuaries.

Scientists have compared the amount of food produced in estuaries with amounts produced by other ecosystems. They found that some estuaries produce twenty times as much food as an equal area of open sea. Salt marshes are especially valuable. Each year an acre of salt marsh produces as much as ten tons of plants and animals. The best wheat lands in the world yield seven tons an acre. Only the most fertile rice and sugar-cane fields produce as much food energy as the most fertile salt marshes. To yield such big crops these fields require people to till the soil and add fertilizer. Salt marshes do not need much help. They are tilled and fertilized by the tides.

A seine full of menhaden, caught off the coast of North Carolina: young menhaden feed and grow up in estuaries.

Estuaries are among the most valuable ecosystems on earth. But many people do not know this. They think of estuaries as smelly, muddy, useless places. They call estuaries "wastelands."

Cities have been built near estuaries because they make good harbors for ships and because rivers serve as watery roads for inland trade. Estuaries have also been handy dumping places for wastes. Chemicals and hot water from industries pour into them.

Wastes from toilets and sinks also flow into estuaries. In small amounts this sewage adds to the food available for estuary animals. But large amounts rob the water of oxygen that animals need. Thick deposits build up on the bottom until oysters have no firm places to attach themselves. Because of pollution, it is no longer safe to eat oysters, clams, and scallops from parts of many estuaries.

People also damage estuaries by filling them in. Soil, rocks, and trash are often dumped in shallow parts of estuaries. Then homes, industries, motels, and airports are built on the filled land.

Trash is often dumped into the valuable shallow water areas of estuaries. Other wastes in the water sometimes make it unsafe to eat oysters and other mollusks.

THIS AREA
CLOSED
TO ALL DIGGING
OF CLAMS, QUAHOGS, MUSSELS
AND OTHER MARINE MOLLUSKS
BECAUSE OF POLLUTION
IT HAS BEEN CERTIFIED THAT CLAMS, QUAHOGS, MUSSELS, OYSTERS AND OTHER MARINE MOLLUSKS IN THIS AREA, "CLOSED AREA NUMBER ," DO NOT CONFORM WITH PUBLIC HEALTH STANDARDS AND REGULATIONS AS ESTABLISHED BY THE STATE OF MAINE AND THE UNITED STATES PUBLIC HEALTH SERVICE.
CLOSED AREA NUMBER
Commissioner of
Sea and Shore Fisheries

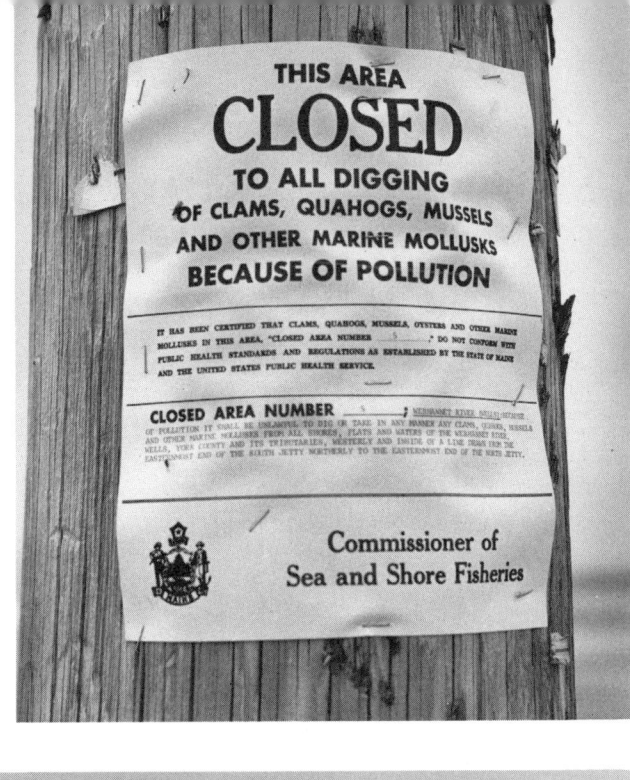

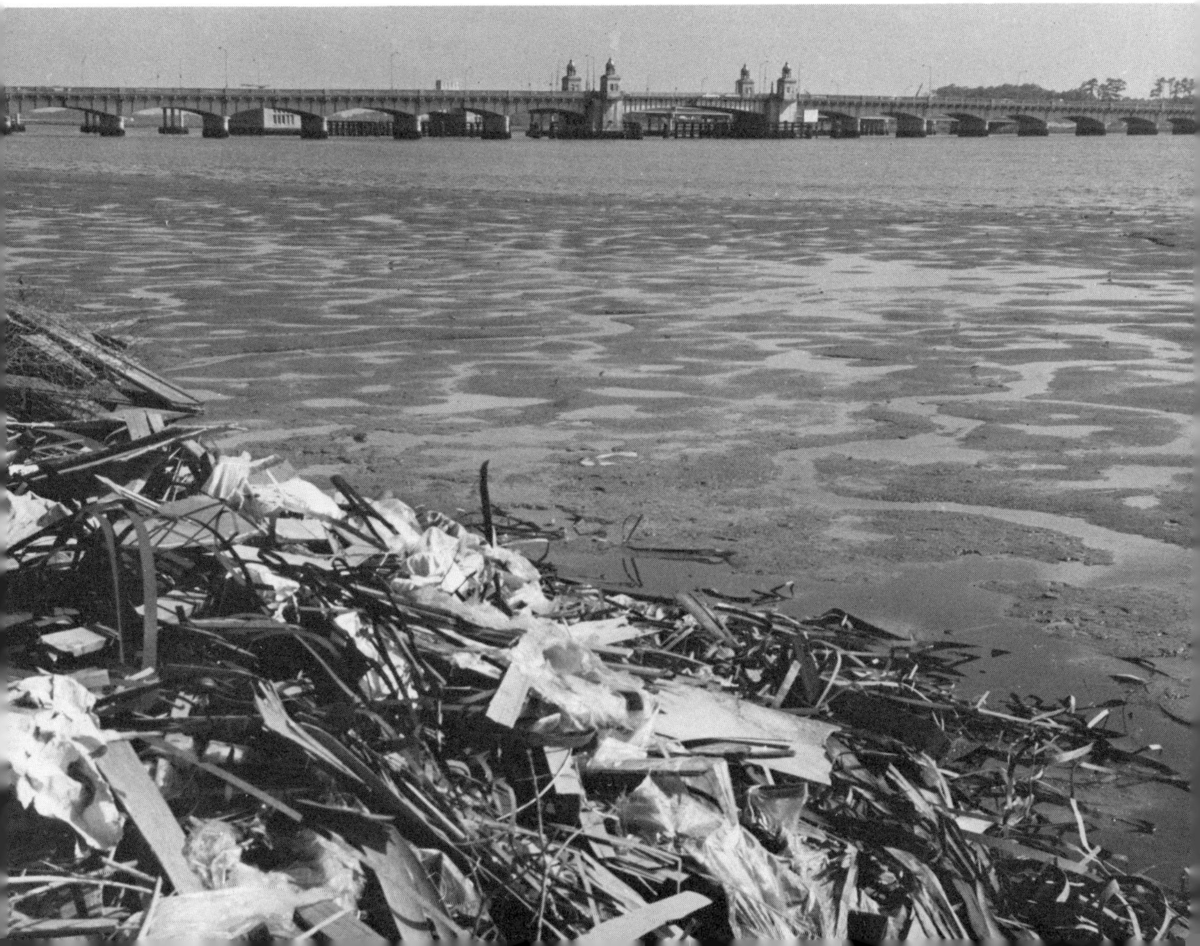

Giant dredges are used to deepen channels for ships and pleasure boats. Sometimes new channels are made. Often the mud and silt that dredges scoop from the bottom is deposited in shallow water, filling it in. A great amount of silt is stirred up. It slowly settles to the bottom again. Oyster beds may be buried, or the oysters may simply die because there is so much silt in the water they filter.

San Francisco Bay is an estuary and it is a good example of one that has been badly damaged by people. A third of the bay has been filled. The remaining water is polluted. San Francisco Bay once produced fifteen million pounds of oysters a year. Now it produces none.

People are trying to save San Francisco Bay from further damage. A government commission has been set up to control changes there. Part of the bay may be protected as a wildlife refuge.

Dredges are used to deepen channels
and to fill in shallow areas so that homes,
highways, and factories can be built.

There are about nine hundred estuaries along the coasts of the United States. They cover twenty-six million acres. About eight million acres are covered with water less than six feet deep. This is the area that is most easily filled, and which has been damaged the most. It is also the most valuable part of the estuaries—the mud flats, eelgrass meadows, and salt marshes that provide food and shelter for so much life.

When one part of an estuary is destroyed or damaged, the whole ecosystem suffers. Fish may be affected in coastal waters far from the estuary. People are hurt too. Fishermen, clam diggers, and crab catchers go out of business. People have to pay more for seafood, or go without. There are fewer places for fishing, swimming, and boating. There are fewer wild animals to see.

People find many clams and other seafood in Great South Bay, south of Long Island, New York. Shallow estuary areas like this are most often damaged or destroyed by people.

Each year thousands of acres of estuaries are destroyed. Plans are being made for more dredging and filling, more power plants, more housing developments. The threats to estuaries are great, and they are growing.

But there is hope. People are beginning to recognize the great value of estuaries. Some salt marshes have been made into wildlife refuges. The federal government

and some state governments are buying more estuary areas. Several states now have laws that help protect estuaries from dredging and filling.

Gulls gather on dredged-up earth where there once was a salt marsh. Rows of houses will soon cover this land. Each year thousands of acres of estuaries are destroyed in this way.

There is hope that estuaries can be saved for the good of people and all life on earth. Estuaries supply food for a hungry world. They provide fishing, boating, and other recreation. They are outdoor laboratories where scientists can study nature. Estuaries are beautiful places of shining waters, lush grasses, and graceful birds.

Estuaries are too valuable to destroy, and people are working to save them.

Common egrets find safety in the salt marshes of Brigantine National Wildlife Refuge. Atlantic City, New Jersey, is in the background.

# GLOSSARY

ALGAE—simple plants that have no roots, stems, or leaves. Some are hundred-foot-long seaweeds. Most are tiny single cells.

BACTERIA—tiny one-celled plants that cannot make their own food. Bacteria aid the decay of dead plants and animals.

CORDGRASSES—two kinds of grass that thrive in the salt marshes of North America. One, called *Spartina alterniflora*, grows to be ten feet tall and has big, coarse leaves. The other, *Spartina patens*, grows no more than two feet high.

CRUSTACEANS—animals in the group Crustacea, which have a hard outer skeleton, no backbone, and paired, jointed limbs. Crustaceans include lobsters, crayfish, crabs, shrimps, barnacles, and sow bugs.

DETRITUS—bits and pieces of anything; in an estuary, bits and pieces of dead plants and animals.

"DROWNED" RIVER VALLEY—a valley carved by a river when the sea level was low, which was then partly filled when the sea rose or the land sank. The water level of the oceans rose about ten thousand years ago when glaciers melted. This "drowned" many valleys, creating estuaries.

ECOLOGY—the study of relationships between living things and their environment.

ECOSYSTEM—a place in nature with all of its living and non-living parts. The earth is one huge ecosystem. Other ecosystems include forests, deserts, ponds, puddles, and rotting logs.

EELGRASS—a saltwater plant that looks like grass. It grows thickly in shallow water and is a source of food and shelter for many animals.

ENVIRONMENT—all of the surroundings of an organism, including other living things, soils, water, and climate.

ESTUARY—a place where salt water and fresh water mix, usually where ocean tides enter a river. Estuaries are usually called bays, sounds, harbors, and lagoons.

FILTER FEEDERS—animals that get their food by straining it from water that passes through part of their bodies. Clams, mussels, and oysters are filter feeders.

FJORD—a narrow, steep-sided valley connected to the sea. Fjords are estuaries and are common along the coasts of Norway and Alaska.

FUNGI—a group of plants that, like bacteria, cannot make their own food. Fungi include yeasts, molds, and mushrooms. They aid the decay of dead plants and animals.

GROUNDWATER—water from rain and melted snow that soaks underground into sand, gravel, and certain kinds of rocks. Groundwater that seeps out along coasts is part of the fresh water that mixes with sea water in estuaries.

LARVAE—the young of some groups of animals, especially insects. Larvae are usually quite active. Young oysters are called larvae during the short time they swim and drift in the water.

MOLLUSKS—a group of animals including more than 80,000 species, most of which are covered with a protective shell. Mollusks include snails, clams, oysters, mussels, squids, and octopuses.

NUTRIENTS—substances needed for normal growth and development of a plant or animal.

POLLUTION—people-produced wastes, such as heat, noise, sewage, and poisons, that lower the quality of the environment.

SALT MARSHES—low, wet, open areas along sea coasts where the main plant life is cordgrasses. The marshes reach as far inland as the tides come and as far into the sea as the marsh plants can survive. Salt marshes produce great amounts of food energy and are among the most valuable ecosystems on earth.

SEDIMENTS—fine material such as sand, gravel, silt, and mud which are carried and then deposited by water, wind, or ice.

SEWAGE—solid and liquid wastes carried in used water from bathtubs, toilets, and sinks.

SILT—soil made up of fine rock particles (finer than sand). Carried along by currents, silt settles to the bottom in quiet waters.

SPAWN—to deposit egg and sperm cells in the water; the way that salmon, trout, and many other kinds of fish reproduce.

TIDES—regular changes in the surface level of ocean waters, caused by the attraction of gravity between the earth and the moon and sun.

# INDEX

*Asterisk ( * ) indicates drawing or photograph*

PICTURE CREDITS

Photographs by Laurence Pringle unless otherwise noted

U.S. Department of Commerce, NOAA, National Marine Fisheries Service:
Bureau of Commercial Fisheries (Bob Williams), 38
Middle Atlantic Coastal Fisheries Center, Sandy Hook Laboratory (Tony Chess), 26, 41 (bottom)
Northeast Atlantic Fisheries Center, Biological Laboratory (Clyde L. MacKenzie, Jr.), 29, 30 (both), 33

Diagrams and map by Jill Schwartz

# ALSO BY LAURENCE PRINGLE

**FOR YOUNG READERS**

*Dinosaurs and Their World*

*The Only Earth We Have*

*From Field to Forest*

*In a Beaver Valley*

*One Earth, Many People:*
  *The Challenge of Human Population Growth*

*Cockroaches:*
  *Here, There, and Everywhere*

*Ecology:*
  *Science of Survival*

*From Pond to Prairie*

*This Is a River*

*Pests and People:*
  *The Search for Sensible Pest Control*

**FOR ADULTS**

*Wild River*